Montessori Insights

for parents of young children

---

*Applying
Montessori Principles
in the Home*

by

Aline D. Wolf

www.parentchildpress.com
1-866-727-3682

Acknowledgments

My thanks to Catherine Maresca for her encouragement, vision and careful editing of this book. I would also like to acknowledge the contributions of the following friends and relatives who read this book in manuscript form and offered useful comments and suggestions: Gerald Wolf, Peggy Curran, Grace Wolf, Mary Martone, Tara Steinbugl, Joan Gilbert, Dorie Wolf, Christopher Wolf, Elizabeth McMeekin, Joanna Johnson, Roxana Gamez, Therese Sullivan, Therese Forbes, Cynthia DeLeon, Barbara Rogers, Jodibeth McCain, Karen Dolan, Wendy Shenk-Evans, Jane Brinley, Isabel Parker and Dawn Fenton.

Book design: Jana Stanford Sidler & Holly Weetman
Photographs: Cynthia DeLeon
and many other Montessori parents
Library of Congress Control Number: 2005922584
ISBN # 978-0-939195-33-6

Dedication

For Peggy Curran—whose expertise has enhanced my
work and whose friendship has enriched my life
for over twenty-five years.

Table of Contents

Introduction

The writings and lectures of Maria Montessori were actually meant for parents as well as for teachers. *Education,* she believed, *is to be regarded as a help to life.*[1] As such, *education must start at birth,*[2] not at six years of age, not even at three years of age. This premise automatically places parents, or those who act in their place, as the child's first and most important teachers.

In addressing a significant portion of her writings to parents, Montessori concentrated on the extraordinary importance of the child's first six years as the foundation for all future learning. *We serve the future by protecting the present,* she wrote. *The more fully the needs of one period are met, the greater will be the success of the next.*[3]

The phenomenal resurgence of Montessori education in North America since 1959 has resulted in several thousand Montessori schools. Many of these were started by parents who were intrigued by Montessori's ingenious educational materials and awed by the comfortable and commendable behavior of three to six year-old children in Montessori classrooms. Although most parents admired the way their children performed in these schools, relatively few of them were able to encourage the same kind of behavior at home.

During this time, Montessori teacher training courses proliferated but very little of Montessori's wisdom was made available for families. Although some Montessori schools provided lectures or study groups for parents of their students, there were virtually no Montessori courses or workshops for parents who could not take advantage of a Montessori school, but might have been open to using Montessori principles at home.

My purpose here is to offer what I consider to be the best of Maria Montessori's insights to today's parents and to suggest how these principles can be applied in a world that is significantly different from the world in which she developed them. The traditional two-parent family of her era is now only one of many family configurations. The stay-at-home mother of Montessori's time is now likely to be a mother, perhaps a single parent, who works outside the home, so that many of the child's waking hours are under the supervision of another relative, baby-sitter, or daycare center.

Additionally, the culture that surrounds and influences these families has been radically altered in recent decades, particularly by unprecedented developments in transportation, technology and communication. Children who once played imaginative games in their immediate neighborhood are now driven to organized sports and events.

Instant communication and electronics pervade many of today's homes and have taken over what used to be family time. Montessori could not have imagined the enormous influence of television, radio, computers, the internet, cell phones, and electronic games on the lives of children. Does her perspective of one hundred years ago apply to families in our highly technological environment?

Despite some outdated elements of her work, I believe that Montessori's most profound insights into the nature of children offer parents a storehouse of wisdom that they can call upon in many everyday situations. Like her classroom materials that are still used daily a century after she designed them, Montessori's principles for the care of the young child are some of the most valuable guidelines we have for child rearing. Because they are based on the true nature of the child, Montessori's theories have a universal quality that has survived the test of generations and proven effective for children of different times, races, cultures, and religions.

Her ingenious insights came from her great gift, the ability to observe children as they really are—not little adults, but unique entities with very special needs, particular ways of learning, and surprising delight in ordinary experiences. *The child has his own laws of development,* she wrote, *and if we want him to grow, it is a question of following these, not of imposing ourselves upon him.*[4]

Essentially this book is about applying Montessori insights at home. It will not tell you when to use vitamin drops or what to do when your child has colic or croup. Neither will it detail what your child should be doing at ten months, how many words she should know at two years, or how three-year-olds differ from four-year-olds. Such details abound in other handbooks for parents.

In the chapters that follow I have used many quotations from Montessori's writings because in this book I want you to hear her voice as well as mine. Her words are in italics, and I have edited some of them for clarity and gender inclusiveness. In addition I have quoted other authors (using quotation marks), whose ideas complement or reinforce the ideas of Montessori.

Complementing the Montessori Classroom

Although this book is addressed to any parent with a child under seven years of age, it may have particular relevance to parents of young children who are currently in or considering a Montessori school. If you are able to use guidelines at home that are similar to those used by your children's teachers, then your children will have the advantage of consistency in their two primary environments. They will not be confused by two sets of standards or conflicting expectations for acceptable behavior. Working alongside the teachers in this way will not only benefit your children, it will enhance your parenting experience and give you the best return on your commitment to Montessori education. No parents should regret that they did not use Montessori insights from their children's earliest days. The key to adopting any different approach is to start where you are now!

The family environment is determined, not by its
structure, but by the substance of every
relationship within the home.

The Importance of Family

Maria Montessori's claim that *education begins at birth* points to the family as the all-important formative environment of the child. The family, no matter how it is structured, totally enfolds every infant and toddler so that they absorb all the sights, sounds, language, tensions, arguments, laughter, and love that surround them.

Each child does this because he has what Montessori calls an *absorbent mind,* a mind quite different from that of an adult, a mind that can literally soak up details from all that he encounters. *The things about him awaken so much interest and so much enthusiasm that they become incorporated in his very existence.*[5] These words challenge us to create a secure and loving family life and caution us against the long-lasting effects of persistent negative circumstances in the home.

For most of us, the basic contours of our lives are set in place by the kind of family life we experience. The family environment is determined, not by its structure but by the substance of every relationship within the home—between adults, between children, and between generations. To nourish these relationships means giving quality time to each one of them. Some adult partners, in an effort to do everything for their children, give little time to their own relationship, thus weakening the foundation that gives security to their children. Because the effects of early home life are long lasting, it seems wise for families to give priority to strengthening and enriching each of these fundamental bonds in order to create a warm, loving and safe atmosphere that will nourish the inner life of each of their children.

In the 1960's Dr. Burton White, head of the Harvard University Pre-school Project, observed that some six-year-olds were well adjusted, competent, self-controlled and eager to learn, while other six-year-olds seemed to lack these beneficial qualities. In an effort to determine what kind of training and opportunities produced the more able six-year-olds, he led a 17-year project in which extensive research was done on thousands of early childhood programs.

First they studied what had influenced these children when they were five, but found that the six-year-olds with these optimal characteristics already had these same qualities when they were five. They found the same results when they studied the nursery schools they had attended when they were four. Finally, they studied how their subjects were as three-year-olds and found that the children who were competent at six had been competent at three. "In the end," Burton White wrote, "we were quite convinced that a long term approach to understanding good develop-

ment had to start with a focus on the first three years of life."

"In our studies we were not only impressed by what some children could achieve during the first years, but also by the fact that the child's own family seemed so obviously central to the outcome. Indeed, we came to believe that the informal education that families provide for their children makes more of an impact on a child's total educational development than the formal educational system. If a family does its job well, the professional can then provide effective training. If not, there may be little the professional can do to save the child from mediocrity."[6]

The First Three Planes of Human Development

Of particular importance to parents is Montessori's basic conviction that the first eighteen years of human development can be divided into three distinct periods, or planes. Each plane involves its own particular characteristics, needs, and styles of learning. The transition from one period to the next is marked not only by physical changes, but also by psychological changes. Adults who understand these functional differences can anticipate them and reciprocate with corresponding modifications in their own style of parenting or supervision.

The first of these periods extends from birth to about six years of age, when the child loses his first set of teeth. One needs only to observe the great difference between a newborn and a six-year-old to realize that this is a phenomenal period. In addition to physical growth, there is also the almost total transformation from a helpless mute infant to a youngster with fully coordinated movements and an impressive command of her native language.

Learning in the early part of this period is directed from within. The adult role is not to teach but to prepare the environment that will facilitate the work of the child's inner teacher. For example, the child, without any coaching, begins to exercise the muscles he will need to perform all the movements of his arms and legs. The adult provides the freedom for this movement. Likewise, if he has no neural deficits, hearing or speech impediments, the child effortlessly absorbs a whole language modeled for him by adults. At the same time, the child constantly explores everything in the environment provided by the adults. As this period draws to a close, the child gradually becomes more responsive to direct instruction.

The second plane of development extends roughly from six to twelve years of age. Compared to the periods preceding and following it, this span of time is one of relative stability marked by steady growth and expansion of knowledge rather than constant change. *Knowledge can best be given where there is eagerness to learn, so this is the period when the seeds of everything can be sown.*[7] The child's implicit "What is this?" question of the first period now becomes "How?" "Why?" "When?" and "Where?" "How does water get to the spigot?" "Why does the moon get bigger and smaller?" "When did the dinosaurs live?" and "Where do babies come from?"

These young explorers want to go beyond the environments of their homes and schools. They delight in nature camps, field trips, science museums, planetarium shows, children's plays, movies, and concerts. They want to be with other children, play sports, and explore questions of right and wrong. Through all these experiences, aided by adults, they gradually acquire a broad variety of basic information, culture, values, and social skills.

The third plane of development begins with puberty and extends to about eighteen; it is also called adolescence. The first half, age 12-15, is often a turbulent period marked by numerous physical changes as the body matures. *The character is seldom stable at this age; there are signs of indiscipline and rebellion.*[8] As she observed their restlessness in traditional classrooms and their desire to become independent from their parents, Montessori proposed that these young teenagers learn best through real experiences requiring considerable physical effort, with some time spent away from home supervised by reliable adults other than family members. In her booklet titled Erdkinder, which means "Land-Children", she calls this *a school of experience in the elements of social life.*[9] In addition to some academics, the *erd-kinder* gives adolescents real work in such activities as carpentry, farming, animal care, and other occupations, as well as opportunities to learn economics by marketing the products of their labor.

Since these very young adults are particularly sensitive to their changing appearance, opinions of their peers, and their place on the popularity scale, some of them may be affected by an inferiority complex, anxiety, or even depression, because to them *the future seems insecure and full of unknown factors.*[10] Nurturing their self-confidence and self-respect becomes a primary concern of supervising adults. *The adolescent must never be treated as a child, for he has surpassed that stage. It is better to treat him as if he had greater value than he actually shows, rather than to treat him as if he had a lower value.*[11]

Finally, in the latter half of this period the restlessness and instability of the earlier years gradually give way to maturity. More adult-like behavior can be expected as he or she may learn to drive a car, accept new responsibilities, actually work to earn money, and be ready for more challenging academic work.

The Importance of the First Plane

Montessori clearly proclaims the first plane of development as the most consequential—the one that has the greatest influence on an individual's total life. *The most important period of life is not the age of university studies, but the first one, the period from birth to the age of six. For that is the time when human intelligence itself is being formed. But not only intelligence; the full totality of psychic powers.*[12]

What does Montessori mean by *psyche* and *psychic powers?* In the <u>American Heritage Dictionary</u> the first meaning for the word *psyche* is "The soul or spirit as distinguished from the body." The second meaning is "The mind functioning as the center of thought, feeling, and behavior, and consciously or unconsciously adjusting and relating the body to its social and physical environment."

Although Montessori herself did not specifically define *psyche*, she used it in the sense of this second definition. She saw the *psyche* unconsciously directing the child toward all he must do and learn in

this first plane of development. *During this early period education must be understood as a help to the unfolding of the child's inborn psychic powers. This means that we cannot use the orthodox methods of teaching, which depend on talk...It is as if nature had safeguarded each child from the influence of adult reasoning, so as to give priority to the inner teacher who animated him.*[13]

Nurturing a child during her first three years requires great respect for this inner teacher. Montessori emphasized its importance repeatedly because even though it cannot be seen or touched, it can be thwarted by adults who are unaware of its existence. Well-meaning parents who are not adequately informed about the strong natural instincts that are vital to children's optimal development, can unwittingly frustrate children's burgeoning efforts by giving unquestioned precedence to their own will, their adult environment and their fast moving schedules. This does not mean that you should relax all discipline and allow your children to do whatever appeals to them. It means becoming informed on the behaviors that are essential to children's development and creating conditions in which they can flourish.

What has to be defended is the construction of human normality... To recognize this great work does not mean to diminish the parents' authority. Once they can persuade themselves not to be the builders, but merely to act as collaborators in the building process, they become much better able to carry out their real duties.[14]

The First Days of Life

Before Montessori's time the care of infants focused on physical considerations. Montessori, however, with her keen sensitivity to the psychological needs of a young child, was deeply concerned about the emotional shock that the newborn undergoes in moving from the environment of the mother's womb to the outside world.

Within the womb the baby floated effortlessly in the amniotic fluid. He experienced only darkness, warmth, and the sounds and motions of his mother's body. Imagine the impact of being born into a brightly lit room, with different sounds and temperature plus the first experience of breathing air. Montessori wrote that in order to minimize distress *the child must remain as much as possible in the first few days in contact with his mother. There must not be too much contrast, as regards to warmth, light and noise, with his conditions before birth.*[15] Obviously the initial shock of entering the world can be lessened if, for the first few days, the child lies against his mother's body in a semi-darkened room. Here he can be readily nourished by her breast milk and comforted by the warmth of her body and the familiar sound of her heartbeat.

We may say that the child has merely changed his position in regard to her: he is now outside her body instead of inside. But everything else remains the same and the communion between them still exists.[16] A quiet period of rest allows both the mother and child to recover from the birth experience and to form a loving and comfortable bond.

Considerations for the Early Months

As the infant gradually becomes accustomed to brighter light, she begins to look around. *The first lesson we must learn,* Montessori writes, *is that the tiny child's absorbent mind finds all its nutrients in its surroundings. Here it...builds itself up from what it takes in. Especially at the beginning of life we must, therefore, make the environment as interesting and attractive as we can.*[17]

Of primary importance is the mother's face. As the mother quite naturally looks directly at the baby, making loving eye contact while smiling, cooing, singing or speaking, the child absorbs her first comforting social contacts. She will soon look at other people and other things around her but will nearly always keep returning to her mother's face for reassurance.

As the child begins to focus her eyes on her surroundings, it is important to have beautiful colorful objects within her field of vision. When a child is kept in a semi-darkened room or a hooded carriage during her waking hours, she is deprived of vital sensory stimulation. Montessori tells us that in a well-designed nursery *the walls are adorned with plenty of pictures, and the child lies on a gently sloping support, so that he can take in the whole scene—and not have his gaze fixed only on the ceiling.*[18]

One of the most tender emotional moments for a new mother occurs when she places her finger in the palm of her baby's hand, and the infant closes his tiny fingers around it. This initial grasping, although unconscious, is one of the first acts of the baby's hand. Within a few months the baby will reach out intentionally to grasp whatever may be near him, such as his mother's hair, or her glasses. *Not until grasping has occurred is the baby's attention drawn to the hand that enabled him to do it. This clutching of objects, which at first was unconscious, now becomes conscious, and, as we see by watching the child, it is his hand and not his foot which first claims his attention. Once this has happened, grasping continues rapidly, and instead of being instinctive, as it was at first, it becomes intentional.*[19] Be sure to provide rattles and soft toys within his reach so he can easily exercise this newly developing power.

How Language Calls the Child

You may be surprised to learn that an infant begins to absorb his native language in the first few months of life, long before he utters his first few words.

In her book, <u>The Absorbent Mind</u>, Maria Montessori asks, *How does it happen that the child learns to speak? How is it that, among the thousands of sounds and noises that surround him, he...reproduces only those of the human voice?*[20] He does not go around ringing like the telephone or barking like the dog, because *the sounds of human speech make a deeper impression on him than any other sounds.*[21] In other words, the human voice causes such an intensity of emotion and so deep an enthusiasm that it sets in motion the invisible powers within him that ultimately lead to speaking a language.

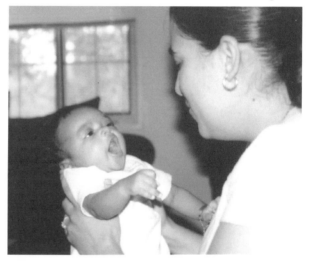

Although you, as parents, do not formally teach your children to speak, you provide a powerful incentive as you model the technique and the vocabulary. So it is important to make eye contact with your infant and to let him watch your lips while you speak clearly and lovingly to him and to name things for him from his earliest days. "This is your shirt." "Now you are going to have your bath." "Now I am kissing your toes." Mumbling, shouting, keeping silence, or speaking with your back turned to him does not stimulate language development and could actually impede it.

Hearing adult conversation helps your child to absorb pronunciation, inflection and grammatical structure. Montessori reminds us that babies in almost every culture have had this opportunity as they were carried upright on their parent's bodies in various shawls, baskets, boards, straps and other means of support. In this advantageous position they absorbed much of their language long before they could speak. Many modern parents replicate this opportunity by carrying their child in a "snuggly" or other support that keeps the baby safely on their chest or back. A baby carried in this way not only absorbs language but also rarely cries because she is close to her parent and constantly fascinated by all that she sees and hears around her.

It is when he hears the full discourse of grown-up people, and can see their actions, which make their meaning clear, that he grasps little by little the construction of sentences. This is far more important than the one-syllable words that his mother lisps to him. It is the language of living thought clothed in action.[22]

As your child's comprehension increases, however, be careful not to conduct inappropriate conversations within her earshot. Don't discuss the child herself, frightening news, negative comments about others, or unsuitable gossip in front of her.

The Importance of Movement

The time that an infant is carried about must also be balanced by opportunities to move all her developing muscles while lying in an unconstrained position. This horizontal position allows the child to kick, arch, roll, creep, and crawl, preparing the mind and muscles for their lifelong tasks. *Human beings, unlike the animals, are not born with movements already coordinated...How different from the young of most mammals, who walk, run and jump from birth, according to their species.*

Humans, instead, bring no such abilities with them into the world, yet their gifts are unsurpassed in learning of movements. Of skilled movements they can acquire the most varied imaginable: those of the craftsman, the acrobat, the dancer, the musician and the champion in the many fields of sport. But none of these things come from a mere ripening of the organs of movement. It is always a matter of experience in action; of practice.[23]

This practice begins in the earliest months. It is a time when a parent who is unaware of the infant's instinctive need to make particular movements, may inadvertently prevent her from doing so. A parent whose concern is to keep the child from kicking off the covers and getting cold may keep the baby wrapped tightly in a blanket or covered with a securely fastened quilt that is impossible to dislodge. Far better to dress the child in a warm but loose-fitting one-piece suit, extending from toes to shoulders, that will enable her to kick freely without becoming cold.

Some pediatricians prefer an infant to sleep on her back because in this position, they believe, crib death is less likely to occur. However, such long hours on her back, where she cannot learn to hold her head up, should be complemented at least twice a day by 15 or 20 minutes of "tummy time" on a blanket on the floor. There she can freely lift her head, kick her legs in a new direction, strengthen hand and arm muscles, and eventually learn to roll over. It is not possible to tell an infant to execute specific movements; parents can only provide the freedom to do so.

Preparing Your Home for a Toddler

Movement seems to explode in the latter half of a baby's first year. When he tries to pull himself up on his hands and knees it is time to assess your home as an environment where a toddler will not only soon be crawling, but also walking, climbing and exploring everything within reach. How can it offer all the experiences the child needs and still be hazard free? Are there any unprotected stairways? Electric wires on the floor? Uncovered low wall sockets? Tablecloths or table scarves that could be easily pulled down? Floor lamps that could be toppled? Sharp corners on tables? Choking hazards?

Are there interesting things for a child to explore and from which she can absorb details? A long mirror mounted horizontally close to the floor? Some lovely pictures, or paintings, (laminated rather than in glass frames) displayed at her eye level? A low window where she can look outside? Age appropriate toys? Beautiful music?

Many first-born children spend their earliest years in a home that was designed primarily for adults. A helpful means to take the perspective of a very young child in the home is to look at adults sitting around a dining room table and then to stoop to the height of a toddler and look at the same scene. The adult sees the faces of the people around the table but the toddler sees only their legs and the legs of the table. When preparing your home for a toddler you may want to sit on the floor in each room to determine what you can put at this level that will be safe, interesting and inviting for a miniature explorer.

Since a young child learns by touching, he has a very strong natural tendency to handle everything in sight. The words, "Don't touch," conflict directly with this vital urge. *The adult environment is not a life-giving environment for the child,* Montessori cautioned. *More often it is an accumulation of obstacles* [24] ...fragile objects within easy reach that he is constantly told not to touch. It is not possible for a child under three to obey a negative command that opposes his strong natural instincts. If he continues to touch a fragile object, despite hearing the command not to touch, breakage may occur and the child is sometimes blamed for what was caused by a delicate object placed inappropriately within his reach. This is particularly true of coffee table items that are at exactly the right height for a toddler. Valuables like vases, candlesticks or carafes must, for a while, be put out of sight and out of reach. When they are reintroduced to your home, talk to the child about the object, what it is for, where it will be kept, and model how to handle it carefully.

Like coffee tables, base cabinets in the kitchen are a part of the home that toddlers naturally like to explore. The door handles, which are actually more suitable for the height of a child than for the height of an adult, seem to invite the child to open these doors and take out the items that are stored there. The parent who anticipates this action can avoid accidents and behavior crises by storing breakable dishes,

sharp instruments and household chemicals in another location not accessible to the child or in a base cabinet that has a childproof latch. Unbreakable items such as metal pots, pans, lids, a flour sifter, paper cups, plastic items like bowls, pitchers, and dishes can provide hours of safe entertainment for a toddler. Some parents also store kitchen toys in a base cabinet so the child can imitate the cook.

There are times when any busy parent must use a playpen or crib to restrict a child for his own safety, but this is best in moderation, balanced by periods of free movement about the house. Fortunately, larger, adjustable enclosures are now available that are much roomier than the old 4' X 4' playpens, and offer a baby, or even twins, a more spacious protected area for crawling and learning to walk. For a few months, as your child is learning to wind his way around hard legs and sharp corners you may want to tape some padding to your furniture rather than severely restrict your toddler's movements.

When an infant begins to crawl, the condition of the floor becomes a factor, as well as small objects, sometimes dropped on the floor, that could be swallowed or cause choking. Since a child of crawling age puts his hands and nearly everything he handles into his mouth, a major effort must be made to eliminate dirt and germs from the floor. It is very helpful if every person who comes into the house promptly removes his or her shoes that carry grime and mud from the streets and fields. Changing into house shoes or slippers keeps outside dirt away from the area where the baby crawls.

Although fear of dirt and germs keep some well-meaning parents from putting a young child on the floor at all, Montessori felt that this restriction of movement delays the child's mental as well as physical development. *The development of his mind comes about through his movements...Observations made on children the world over confirm that the child uses his movements to extend his understanding.*[25] Be careful not to let concern for your home environment or your own activities restrict your toddler from the free exercise that optimizes his physical and mental development.

Sensitive Periods

Once the child begins moving about, her development proceeds at quite a rapid pace. In fact, her accomplishments in the first three years are phenomenal. Think of all she learns in this comparatively brief period. Most remarkably she learns an entire language—the vocabulary, pronunciation, inflection, sentence structure and meaning. She learns to sit up, to stand, to walk, to run, to jump, to climb steps, to lift, to push, to grasp, to feed herself, and to use the bathroom. She knows people's names and understands the purpose of cars, toasters, ovens, showers, telephones, washers, dryers, and many other items in the home. In this initial period children learn more than in any other three year span in their lives, and if no physical or mental problems intervene, they remember this knowledge and these skills for the rest of their lives.

All this happens without any formal teaching because the child in this period has a unique aptitude, an internal guidance system that leads her to each new step in development. She does this, Montessori tells us, by passing through a series of *sensitive periods.* These are intervals of intense fascination for something in the environment needed to learn a particular skill, such as crawling, walking, running, climbing, lifting, and pushing. A spotlight seems to shine on certain parts of the environment that will help the child, such as a sloping path, doors, drawers, water faucets, buttons, and shoes. When the mastery is complete the "spotlight" goes off. It is easier for a child to perfect a particular skill during the corresponding sensitive period than at any other time in her life.

You may notice any number of sensitive periods during which your child takes delight in repeating a particular movement. One of our sons had a strong sensitive period for turning on light switches when he was two and one half years old. He would climb up, in any way he could, and with great excitement flick the wall switch on and off. For the switches that he couldn't reach, we discovered him using a long thin cylinder from his set of blocks to push the switch up to the "on" position. It was a period when we had to go frequently from room to room turning off the lights that he seemed compelled to turn on.

When one of our daughters was about four years old she had a sensitive period for buttoning and unbuttoning. Whenever I wore a particular blue dress that had buttons all the way down the front, I would have to stand still for five minutes or so while she opened and then buttoned the lowest buttons on the dress.

When an adult performs a particular action, such as going upstairs, it is usually for a specific purpose, perhaps to get something that is on the second floor. But during a sensitive period a child will climb the stairs because she is guided by an inner impulse to practice that particular movement. *Staircases give the greatest joy,* Montessori wrote, *because children have in themselves an innate tendency to go upwards.*[26] To come down the stairs is more difficult, and the parent usually has to help the child with this maneuver. The child may then climb the steps again to the chagrin of her caregiver, who may not understand that she is inwardly motivated to master this skill.

Montessori reminds parents that *this kind of activity, which serves no external purpose, gives children the practice they need for coordinating their movements.*[27] The child is fortunate whose parents can perceive the long-range purpose of this kind of repetition and patiently give their time and any necessary assistance.

Gaining Independence

Montessori's chapter on independence in <u>The Absorbent Mind</u> begins with the words, *Except when he has regressive tendencies, the child's nature is to aim directly at functional independence.*[28] He first becomes independent from his mother's womb, then from her breast milk; from being carried to being able to walk; from being fed to feeding himself; from being dressed to dressing himself and so on. *If we observe natural development with sufficient care we see that it can be defined as the gaining of successive levels of independence.*[29]

Sensitive periods play a large part in the child's quest for independence. It is important for caring adults to recognize the signs for each of these various steps in independence, especially the ones for self-care. For example, if you are spoon-feeding a child, who keeps trying to grab the spoon, it is probably a sign that he is ready to try using the spoon by himself. Once you recognize this readiness as a sensitive period, you can help by allowing extra time for his first awkward efforts. Begin by offering him foods that are easily spooned such as applesauce, pudding and mashed vegetables. Since his early attempts at this task will probably result in a messy situation, you can avoid frustration if the child wears easily washed clothes and sits in a chair with a tray or at a low table that can readily be wiped clean. Dressy clothes and lovely tablecloths are for adult pleasure, not for the essential work of the child.

Independence in eating can be fostered first by offering your child finger foods such as flakes of dry cereal, crackers, pieces of banana, small pieces of cheese, and even small lumps of scrambled eggs. Picking these up and putting them in his mouth helps to coordinate the small muscles in his hand.

Small-sized utensils not only intrigue him, they can ease the way to serving himself independently. He is usually more eager to drink his milk or juice if he can pour it himself from a two-ounce size pitcher into a small cup with handles. Also when he is ready to eat cold cereal with a spoon, he can pour it into a bowl from a small cereal box that holds one serving. Then he can pour milk on the cereal, using the same small pitcher.

We can only rejoice each time he shows us a new level of independence ...But...this progress of the child can nevertheless be held back, or slowed down, by any failure to obtain the needed environ-

mental experiences.[30] Not every parent will have the time, particularly in the morning rush, to allow the child to do all these things independently. However, if you recognize their importance, you will allow him to do at least one of them while you do the others. Then in the evening, on weekends, or days when you do not have to go to work, you can allow more time for these developmental steps.

Dressing herself is a major step toward independence for a young child. It will not happen all at once but in a series of little successes. At first she may be able to put on her own slippers, then her socks. Shoes that are fastened with Velcro allow independence for young children until they are ready to learn the more challenging skills of lacing and tying. When buying shirts, blouses, dresses, nightgowns, or even an apron for a young child, remember that those that fasten in the front will facilitate independence. If the buttons, zippers or snaps are in the back, the child will have to depend on someone else to fasten them. When she buttons them herself, show her how to start with the bottom button and work upward. This will help her to match each button with its corresponding buttonhole.

The child's first instinct is to carry out his actions by himself, without anyone helping him, and his first conscious bid for independence is made when he defends himself against those who try to do the action for him.[31] This defense often leads to frustration for both parents and children when a child desperately wants to do it himself but is not yet able. On the other hand, there are some who do not want to try to dress themselves because they may really think they cannot do it. Whether your child is frustrated or reluctant to try, you can assume the role of helper. "If you put one arm in the sleeve of your coat by yourself, I will help you with the other one." "If you put your toes into your shoe, I will help you push your heel in."

If she has trouble fastening small buttons and zippers, let her practice on larger ones on an adult jacket or coat. If this is not effective then sew one large button on a piece of fabric and cut a corresponding size buttonhole on another. Be sure this buttonhole is roomy enough to slip the button through it easily.

Many children are more willing to dress themselves if they can choose what they want to wear. To avoid inappropriate choices, put two or three selections of clothes suitable for the day's activity in a low drawer and let her make the choice. Dressy clothes or those that are out of season can be kept elsewhere. Allowing children to dress themselves completely may not be possible on mornings when you are rushed. Some parents who are convinced of the value of children learning to dress themselves have solved this dilemma by having the children do some of this the night before when there is more time. After their baths, the children can put on their clean underwear, select their clothes for the next day and lay them out carefully ready to be put on. Other parents told me their children put all their clothes on the night before. When they sleep in the clothes they are going to wear the next day, they have only their shoes to put on in the morning rush.

Another way to foster your child's independence is to hang a mirror at her height. Then rather than ordering her to "Come here so I can wash your face," you can say, "Look in your mirror and see if your face needs any attention."

When she is capable of washing her face and hands and/or cleaning her teeth, put a step stool beside the bathroom sink, so she can reach the water without having to ask for adult help.

You may wonder why helping a child to act independently is so important. Look at it this way. If you do everything for him, it gives him the message "You can't do it yourself." He will not only lack the experience that gives him competence, but he may also lose confidence in his own ability. A great deal of learning in school depends on a child's confidence to try new things. If he has not built up confidence in himself, he will be more likely to think or say, "I can't do it." Giving him encouraging messages like, "I know you can do it yourself" in his early years helps to strengthen his will to tackle the new learning tasks he will meet in school. *As soon as independence has been reached, the adult who keeps on helping becomes an obstacle.*[32] Why not post these words of Montessori in a place where you will see them every day?

What About Order?

Contrary to what many parents believe about children, Montessori claims that *the child's need for order is one of the most powerful incentives to dominate his early life.*[33] Somehow, in America, childhood has become almost synonymous with disorder, as bedroom floors are covered with clothing and playrooms look like holding tanks for the scattered remains of broken toys. Such unkempt environments not only overwhelm the child, they frustrate him in his efforts to find meaningful experience.

If we watch carefully, as Montessori did, children will give us signs that they are more comfortable in an ordered environment and with a regular routine. When playing they make orderly arrangements of rooms in a dollhouse or rows of little cars in a toy garage and they put their stuffed animals to bed every night with the same little blankets. They are often deeply disturbed, as our children were, when a sizable piece of furniture in the living room has been moved to a different location, or when they learn that the family has acquired a new couch and the old familiar one is gone. As Montessori says, *The child often feels the deepest impulse to bring order to what, according to his logic, is in a state of confusion.*[34]

To nourish this burgeoning sense of order, it is wise for parents to have a comfortable system of tidiness in the child's environment from his earliest years. This means keeping his clothing items and toys to a manageable number with specific places for his things to be kept. When you undress him let him watch you and hear you say, "I am going to put your dirty clothes in the hamper: or "I am going to hang this shirt here so you can wear it again tomorrow." Then when he learns to walk, he knows the routine and he can put the clothes to be washed in the hamper by himself, or put his shirt on a low hook to be worn again. Thus, from his earliest years, orderly habits can be encouraged. As he grows, you will want to install more low hooks for his jacket, cap, pajamas and other clothing. Later a bar at his shoulder height in the closet will enable him to reach clothes that are hung on hangers.

Besides the bottom drawers for his clothing, mentioned earlier, low shelving is a great help for keeping toys and books in order. The Montessori classroom for three to six year-olds is filled with shelves within easy reach of the children. Each piece of learning material has its own assigned place on one of these shelves. Even the three year-olds quickly learn where each piece of material belongs, and after using it, they are quite willing to return it to its proper place on the shelf.

The key to this orderly behavior both in the classroom and at home is having enough accessible shelving for the number of things to be stored and helping children to keep their things in place. The large toy chest used in many homes does not contribute to a sense of order because toys are thrown into it at random. When a child is looking for a toy that is at the bottom of the chest, everything on top of that toy is usually thrown out on the floor.

It is best if the number of toys does not exceed the limits of the storage capacity within reach of your child. Not every toy has to be on a shelf. For example, tricycles can be kept on the porch or in a garage. Balls or blocks can be stored in baskets. Stuffed animals can be on the child's bed; a music box on a windowsill—just so each thing has a place.

Children who have too many toys rarely value them or care for them. Indeed they often miss the joy of having a favorite toy that they treasure. Therefore, removing toys from the child's environment is just as important as providing them. If your children have more toys than you have space for, put some away for rainy days, long car trips, or periods of illness. Rotating toys in and out of storage often creates new interest in them. When new toys are added, encourage your child to give older toys in good condition to a younger family member or to a toy collection for families who cannot afford to buy them.

Orderliness in the home can be more difficult to maintain than in the classroom. Look at it as an ongoing process rather than something you expect to achieve very quickly. There will be some days when most of your children's things are in order. There will be other days when you know you have to help them put their things back in place. And yes, there will be days when chaos reigns. However if you understand the value of order for your children, you will keep it as a significant goal in your parenting.

Order is not only desirable for children's things, it is equally important for their routines. Do you have a ritual for going out and coming home? A hug? A kiss? Do you have regular hours for meals? Does each child have his own place at the table and in the car? If you have grace before meals, is it said regularly with each one participating? In the morning do the children eat before dressing or dress before eating? Children are more comfortable and compliant if there are established routines. Try to be faithful to whatever customs you establish for your children and prepare them ahead of time for any necessary short-term changes.

This is particularly true for bedtime rituals, which will differ in various families, but are most effective if they are consistent within each home. A nightly bath, brushing teeth, night prayers, putting a doll to bed, saying good-night to each person in the family, playing a music box or a lullaby tape, turning on the night light, listening to a story or a favorite book and, of course, hugs and kisses. Nightfall is a time when some children feel insecure. They may be afraid of the dark or afraid to be left alone in bed. A pleasurable routine with an established order of activities is not only reassuring but also a ritual they can look forward to at the end of each day.

Rituals are also important for annual celebrations such as birthdays, holidays, and vacations. They help young children enjoy these events rather than be disturbed by the change of their routines. The fondest memories of many children are of the family's ritual celebrations. *Order is one of the needs of life which, when it is satisfied, produces a real happiness.*[35]

Reading to Your Child

A most delightful and beneficial routine is reading to your child. Cuddling her on your lap or sitting side by side with your arm around her while you read aloud, immediately lets her associate reading with pleasure.

How old must a child be before you start to read to him? Jim Trelese in his wonderful <u>Read-Aloud Handbook</u> says, "If the child is old enough to talk to, he's old enough to be read to. It's the same language."[36] Nearly all parents talk to their babies, so reading to your child can begin in infancy. Begin with simple books of pictures. Then introduce books of rhymes or songs that will delight a child's sensitivity for the rhythm and rhyme of language. Until he begins to understand the meaning of what you are reading, it is only the sound of the language that will appeal to him.

When he is old enough to touch the book you are reading, choose books with special features, such as various textures, peepholes and flip-ups. Watch his delight as he responds to these sensorial elements. As he gets older you can make the sounds of various animals in the stories and he can point to the corresponding illustrations. Eventually he will want to grasp the book you are reading and perhaps hold it himself. This is the time for soft chunky books, perhaps made of cloth, or board books that cannot be easily torn, even if he turns the pages. Respect for books should be a constant in your routine. "We are going to hold this book very carefully and turn the pages one at a time." "Now that we have finished reading we are going to put this lovely book right here (out of reach if he is likely to tear it) so we can read it again tomorrow night."

Above all, read rhymes over and over to your child. A good source of these is Jack Prelutsky's <u>Read-Aloud Rhymes for the Very Young</u> or the <u>Lucy Cousins Book of Nursery Rhymes</u> (Dutton Publishers). If you continue this habit on a daily basis, your child will never be able to remember a day that he did not enjoy contact with a book.

According to Jim Trelese, reading aloud to children exposes them to three times as many vocabulary words as simply talking to them.[37] Words like "nimble," "fiddle," "contrary," and "bunting" are all in the Mother Goose Rhymes and "hippopotamus," "princess," "raggedy," "sixpence," and "coward" are in other poems and stories for children, but probably not in your everyday conversation. Therefore, this special one-on-one activity with your child can enrich the vocabulary she is absorbing effortlessly during this six-year sensitive period for acquiring language.

Your children may ask you to read the same book aloud time after time. While this may bore you, remember that your children love repetition, and are gradually memorizing nursery rhymes, short poems and other favorite lines that they may remember throughout their lives.

Reading is at the heart of all education, because the learning of almost every subject in school—even math—depends on this skill. The habit of reading to your child will not necessarily teach him to read but it nearly always inspires him to want to read. Such a strong desire both eases the way to mastering this skill and starts a valuable lifelong habit. How long should you continue reading to your child? The National Commission on Reading recommends reading to a child throughout elementary school, long after he has learned to read by himself.[38] A child's reading ability and his listening ability differ significantly. He may read at a second grade level but listen at a fourth or fifth grade level. Since his own reading at second grade level will not stimulate his level of understanding, he thrives from that special time with you, as you read increasingly challenging books to him.

Besides reading to your child, it is vital that you read yourself as a role model. Jim Trelese warns that the odds are against a child whose role models at home are seldom, if ever, seen or heard reading books for their own information or pleasure.[39]

When your child is about four years old, take him to the public library where he can observe you selecting books for yourself. Then go to the children's section and pick out a small selection of books suitable for him. Let him choose two or three of these to take home. The Read-Aloud Handbook includes an extensive list of books appropriate for children of specific ages.

Nurturing Concentration

There is very little, if any, learning without concentration. In the Montessori classroom for three to six year-olds, lengthening each child's attention span is a long-range purpose of nearly every activity. For example if a child is doing the dishwashing exercise, she is not only having a sensorial experience with the water, improving her coordination, and learning to follow a sequence of actions, but, most importantly, she is extending her concentration on one activity to ten or fifteen minutes. Respect for each child's attention is very evident throughout the room, as a Montessori teacher rarely interrupts a child who is focused on her work.

Cultivating a child's power of concentration actually begins before the child is three. Concentration is a fragile mind-set that can easily be interrupted by adults who do not understand that age 0-3 is the formative stage for this lifelong power. For example, a young child may be floating sticks in a puddle or lining up pots and pans on the kitchen floor when her caretaker decides, "Enough of this mess," and abruptly ends the activity.

To interfere with a child's concentration in order to change his messy clothes or clean up a cluttered floor is to put appearances ahead of the child's psychic development. *If a child's cycle of activity is interrupted, the results are a deviation of behavior, aimlessness and loss of interest...So whatever intelligent activity we witness in a child—even if it seems absurd to us...we must not interfere; for the child must be able to finish the cycle of activity on which his heart is set."* [40]

Although deep respect for concentration is the ideal, there are times in every family when a child's activity must be brought to an end—such as when dinner is ready or it is time to leave for daycare or school. When this happens it is best to alert the child ahead of time or give an alternative. "Five more minutes to build with your blocks." After five minutes you can say, "Do you want help putting away your blocks or can you do it yourself?" Or "I know you are trying to finish your puzzle but it is almost time to go. You may leave it there on the floor and finish it after school."

Because *no one acting on the child from outside can cause him to concentrate,* [41] Montessori cautions us to take special care of a child's spontaneous periods of concentration. If you frequently encroach on them, this essential tool for learning may not flourish. If nurtured, seeds of concentrated activity can blossom, in time, into healthy periods of work and study.

Intelligence and the Hand

For young children concentration requires the purposeful use of their hands. *The hands are the instruments of human intelligence...All people resemble one another in the way they use their feet. But no one can tell what any one person will do with his hands...If early humans had used only speech to communicate their thoughts...no traces would remain of past generations. It is thanks to the hand, the companion of the mind, that civilization has been preserved.* [42]

Unlike the feet, that are limited to such physical activities as walking, running, climbing, kicking, dancing, and skating, the hands have infinite possibilities for a child's future. Every vocation from a seamstress to a surgeon, from a scientist to a concert pianist, from a cook to a mechanic, computer operator, painter, sculptor, involves hands that are well coordinated and practiced. *The more delicate the work,*

Montessori writes, *the more [the manual skill] needs the care and attention of an intelligent mind to guide it.*[43]

Because she was so moved by the vital connection she observed between the hand and the mind, all the learning materials that Montessori designed for the classroom require purposeful manipulation. *The child's intelligence can develop to a certain level without the help of his hand. But if it develops with his hand, then the level it reaches is higher and the child's character is stronger...If his hand wishes to work we must provide him with things on which he can exercise an intelligent activity.*[44]

Through their hands, children can experience the difference between hard and soft, hot and cold, liquid and solid, rough and smooth (daddy's whiskers and mommy's cheeks), or heavy and light. Little ones using their hands to squeeze Play-doh, to string beads, to wrap a doll in a blanket, or to make a magnificent structure with building blocks, are beginning to understand that their hands can change the world.

All Montessori's emphasis on the necessity of appropriate manual activities for young children leads to the importance of tasks in the home that allow the intelligent use of children's hands. (See box on page 27)

The Work of the Child

Perhaps the essence of Montessori's theories on this subject can be expressed by her insight that an *adult works to perfect the environment, but a child works to perfect being itself.*[45] No one can do the child's work for him. He must do it himself in order to become a competent adult. Many adults, who may be wearied and bored by their own labor, feel that young children should not be encouraged to work; they should only play during their earliest years. Those who

feel this way do not understand what Montessori means by the child's work. It is not drudgery. A child's work is to create the adult he or she will become. Each little task, especially if it is self-chosen, contributes to his development. *From this we may infer that the child will enjoy doing the work needed to complete himself. The child's life is one in which work... begets joy.*[46]

This does not mean that a child should never play. Play is a vital part of a child's life. A young child usually doesn't differentiate between play, such as having a doll's tea party and actually working at such a task as sweeping up crumbs. Montessori believed that sometimes even more than play, children enjoy challenging tasks that increase their concentration, coordination, competence and ultimately their independence.

The child's interest in work comes about through his tendency to imitate what his parents and older siblings are doing. One often hears the cry, "Let me do it," from a child who scarcely seems old enough to perform the task. You may see little ones trying to push a vacuum cleaner, move furniture or lift a heavy bag. *He imitates not because someone has told him to do so, but because of a deep inner need which he feels.*[47]

When a child exhibits this kind of behavior, it is the ideal time to let her work along with you, particularly in the kitchen, a sensorial haven for children with good things to smell, taste and feel. When you are cooking, doing laundry, cleaning, gardening, washing the car, or other everyday tasks, let your child join in. The habit of cleaning up after any task will be easier to establish if you provide small tools—broom, mop, carpet sweeper, sponge, dustpan and brush—appropriate for your child's size and strength.

Modern shortcuts in the kitchen, as well as mechanized car washes, power mowers, and other conveniences, eliminate many of the opportunities for children to join in. However, the child's need to do these tasks has not changed. It is still important to arrange situations in which your child can imitate your actions and work with you at everyday tasks.

If we were to establish a primary principle, it would be to constantly allow the child's participation in our lives. For he cannot learn to act if he does not join in our actions, just as he cannot learn to speak if he does not hear...To extend to the child this hospitality, to allow him to participate in our work, can be difficult, but it costs nothing. Our time is a far more precious gift than material objects.[48]

Let Your Child. . .

Scrub potatoes

Scrape carrots

Put peanut butter on celery

Make meatballs

Roll pie dough

Beat eggs

Grease pans

Use a cookie cutter

Decorate cookies

Arrange flowers in a vase

Fold napkins

Match socks

Dust baseboards and windowsills

Wash the car bumpers

Water plants

Selecting Toys

Parents who are following Montessori theories in their home usually try to select toys that are consistent with her principles. Toys that invite the child into an activity have a distinct advantage over those that require him to simply push buttons. Many of the substantial playthings that have been loved by generations of children are preferable to electronic or battery operated toys.

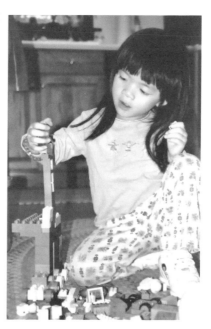

Some days children are more content to play with such simple everyday items as band-aids, stickers, ribbon, or an old deck of playing cards than they are with expensive commercial toys.

Just as the materials in the Montessori classroom are attractive and well made, children's toys at home should be carefully chosen, attractive and safe. This means avoiding flimsy toys or those that have sharp edges, are easily broken, or have many small parts that can be lost or swallowed. Children are often inconsolable when the gear, light bulb or voice box of their new toy doesn't work.

Creative Indoor Play

Dolls	Finger-paints
Doll clothes	Play-Doh
Dollhouses	Crayons
Dress-up box	Play kitchen
Beads to string	Cars and trucks
Building blocks	Puzzles
Pull toys	Play scarves (18 inch silk squares in a variety of colors)
Large cardboard boxes	

Since Montessori endeavored through her work with children to form peace-loving individuals, it is fair to say that she would not have considered guns, swords, or other battle gear as appropriate toys. Montessori warns that *children become like the things they love.*[49]

Sometimes grandparents, other relatives or friends may give your children toys that you feel are not fitting or do not reflect your family values. When this happens, don't be afraid to exchange an inappropriate gift for a more suitable item, even at the risk of offending the gift-giver. Remember that you are the keeper of the home environment and your children's well-being comes first! Such uncomfortable situations can usually be averted if you discuss your guidelines with potential gift givers or suggest the kinds of toys that your child would welcome. Toys that are carefully chosen and maintained can be a source of many hours of sound development as well as fun.

Healthful Outdoor Activities

Climbing bars
Swing
Tricycle
Scooter
Bicycle
Sandbox
Sand toys
Sidewalk chalk
Small Hoola Hoop
Sled or saucer
Skates
Wagon
Balls (all kinds)
Digging tools
Jump rope
Wadingpool
  (supervised)

What About Television?

Maria Montessori did not write about, nor even experience, the enormous influence of television that was just beginning at the time of her death in 1952. We can only speculate what her thoughts would have been on the modern viewing habits of young children. However, looking at these viewing habits in the light of her most important insights on child development lends validity to such speculation.

In recent years television has been blamed for many problems of children of all ages: obesity because the time spent watching TV greatly decreases the time for normal exercise; aggressive behavior because of the violent content of many TV shows; lower academic achievement because, as Jane Healy reminds us, "Research clearly shows that better students tend to watch less. Moreover as viewing goes up, academic scores eventually go down."[50]

More pertinent to this book, however, is taking a look at TV viewers under six years of age who are, according to Montessori, in a major sensitive period for their psychic development. How does TV viewing affect the following aspects of their development?

USE OF THE HANDS: Montessori tells us *that the hands are instruments of human intelligence.*[51] It is not unusual to see a young TV watcher sucking her thumb, twisting her hair, biting her nails or some other perversion of the need to move her hands. In watching TV there is no opportunity for purposeful use of the child's hands to assimilate any new concepts that she is encountering.

LANGUAGE: Montessori placed great emphasis on the unique opportunity for effortless language development in a child's first six years. To capitalize on this opportunity, a child must not only hear a wide variety of words and sentences, but must have practice in using them. Television is like a monologue that gives children little or no opportunity to respond or to ask questions. Furthermore Jim Trelese writes, "The vocabulary of television is lower than nearly all forms of print, from comic books to children's books, newspapers and magazines."[52]

Does this lack of variety and complexity in children's TV scripts lead to the lackluster vocabulary and fragmented sentences used today by many elementary and high school students? Talking to children, reading to them, or telling them stories provides much richer language experiences than television during these critical years.

EXPERIENCE OF REALITY: Montessori believed that young children should experience reality, such as animals in a petting zoo, rather than interpretations of reality, such as cartoons of animals on television. She felt that a young child's development was optimized when he built his perceptions on direct experience as a foundation for upcoming years of curiosity, exploration, invention, and creativity in the arts and sciences. This means that his initial experiences must be rooted in the real world.

The importance of nurturing the child's imagination with the reality of the world can hardly be overemphasized. Every scientific discovery, exploration of our planet or of space, every cure for disease, every novel, poem, symphony, painting, sculpture, and building is a product of someone's imagination put into perceivable form. Montessori emphasizes its importance, *Scientific vision of the truth has not been reached solely by the help of the microscope, but because man's mind is creative...It is by imagination...that all science and all discovery derive their impulse.*[53]

The first seven years are ideal to stimulate a child's imagination and provide means for it to be activated. Playing house allows children to imaginatively recreate experiences they are familiar with. Storytelling in the home encourages children to imagine the characters and scenes in the story. Television, on the other hand, deadens creativity during these important years because the images are already created for the viewers.

According to Joseph Chilton Pearce, "The major damage of television has little to do with content: Its damage is neurological...TV floods the infant-child brain with ready-made images at the very time his or her brain is supposed to learn to make images from within."[54] This inadequacy begins to show on the playground. Where children used to play imaginative games, now they frequently mimic scenes from TV.

CONCENTRATION: Many kindergarten and elementary teachers complain that it is now more difficult to teach children to read than it was in past years. Attention deficit disorders, that seem to have arrived with the era of children's TV watching, are now more prevalent than ever before. These disorders are essentially an inability of school age children to concentrate—the power that Montessori felt should have been carefully nurtured and extended in their first six years. Teachers as well as developmental psychologists have speculated that this difficulty occurs because the brains of children have become accustomed to the fast moving TV images that change every six or seven seconds.

Some research has suggested that the amount of difficulty experienced by six- and seven-year-olds in learning to read is in proportion to the number of hours per day that these youngsters watched TV when they were under four years old.[55] This influence on the development of children's brains needs further professional study, but the possibility of such an effect supports the recommendation of the American Academy of Pediatrics that children two years and under watch no television at all and older children should not have sets in their bedrooms.[56]

REAL NEEDS vs. IMPLANTED DESIRES: Montessori believed that young children have a basic need to form relationships with people. They need loving eye contact; they need to converse with others; they need physical contact from loving caretakers; they need to move about in the real world.

In contrast to such actual experience, frequent television watching creates an unreal environment in which induced desires are fostered by advertisements that promote the interests of large corporations. Brian Swimme tells us, "Before a child enters first grade he will have soaked in thirty thousand advertisements."[57] The message the children hear over and over is that they can attain significance by having what the ad implies everyone else has—certain cereals, soft drinks, athletic shoes, candy bars, and the latest toys and games. This kind of advertising not only deliberately promotes nagging; it makes even the most lovable and talented children feel inadequate or deprived if they cannot have the items that are advertised. In supermarkets and toy stores one can hear children pestering for highly advertised products that are of questionable nutritional or developmental value. Although parents are annoyed with this nagging, many of them ultimately give in to it, thus responding to implanted desires of the child rather than their essential needs.

Controlling Television in Your Home

Despite the many drawbacks of television, it has become a fixture in nearly every child's home. Although some parents of young children can feel proud that by choice they do not own a TV set, most families have not only one, but even three or four sets in their homes. Like driving, TV may be an accepted part of daily life but not appropriate for young children. The problem therefore becomes one of postponing TV watching until a child is more mature. This delay is vital for all children but is particularly important for those under six years of age. Some thoughtful parents have told me of various guidelines they use for controlling TV in the family rather than allowing it to regulate family time and activities.

- No TV viewing for children under two.

- No use of TV as a babyminding tool.

- No TV watching on the nights before the children must get up early to go to school or daycare.

- No TV before leaving for school or daycare in the morning.

- No TV during mealtime, family game time, outdoor play time, or short visits from grandparents, aunts, uncles and family friends who want to interact with the children.

- Limit TV watching to two or three hours per week.

- Carefully record good TV programs and eliminate the advertising.

- Allow young children to watch only videotapes that you have previously viewed and approved.

- Watch TV with your children so that you can discuss what is happening on the screen.

- Search, particularly on public broadcasting, for the best children's programs. Contrary to popular belief, Jane Healy tells us, "Sesame Street is not educationally valuable" and "gives children an erroneous message about what learning feels like."[58] In contrast to this she writes, "Testimony to the fact that a children's program can follow sound development guidelines and still be enduringly popular comes from Mister Rogers' Neighborhood, whose slow repetitive speech and invitations to the child to respond appeals instinctively to preschoolers, at least those whose sensibili ties have not been dulled by raucous sideshows."[59] It is hoped that many of the episodes of the late Fred Rogers will continue in reruns.

- Limit TV sets to the most common areas of the home so children are not watching TV alone and unsupervised.

Discipline

Discipline, Montessori believed, is a gradual unfolding of all the child's powers leading to the very desirable state of self-discipline. Many adults equate the word "discipline" with "punishment," but the real meaning of the word "discipline" is "training." *We must aim at cultivating the will, not breaking it.*[60] In the home as well as in the Montessori classroom, this means training with love, consistency and understanding of a young child's natural impulses.

Before a child is three he cannot obey unless the order he receives corresponds with one of his vital urges.[61] For example, the child at this age has a natural tendency to climb and is likely to ignore an adult

who says, "Don't climb up there." The parent who understands the conflict that this creates for the child, will allow the climbing, unless it is physically dangerous for the child, in which case the parent can try to interest him in a safer climbing experience. No punishment is appropriate here because the child was following a strong natural urge.

As she gets a little older, the child may be able to obey one time but not the next time. Some parents regard this as deliberate disobedience. Montessori however, compares this to the child learning to walk. On one day she may be able to take five or six steps but falls down the next day when she tries. In the same way she may only occasionally follow adult directions because she is in the process of developing her ability to listen to and carry out the will of others.

The parents' attitude, expressed by the tone of voice used, is the key to effective training in the home. Children are human beings, and deserve our respect. Modeling respect for our children and all people will help the child to respect himself and others. Treat your children as respectfully as you would an adult guest in your home. For example, what would you say to a guest at your table who accidentally spills his drink? Would you be as gracious to your own children?

The best time to train a child in good manners and acceptable conduct is not at the time of a behavioral crisis but on a day when he is calm and cooperative. You can have fun role playing "Please," "Thank You," "Excuse Me," "I'm sorry," telephone etiquette, using a handkerchief, covering his nose and mouth when coughing or sneezing, and holding the door for another person. You can also explore being respectful toward people who are different, such as people from other cultures who dress differently, people of different races, people with handicaps or disfigurements. If parents prepare children ahead of time, embarrassing situations can be avoided.

Anticipation is also effective in preventing destructive behavior. For example, many children thoughtlessly destroy vegetables or flowers in the garden by tramping on them or pulling them up. Astute parents can forestall such actions by allowing their child to share in the gardening activities. If he helps to plant seeds, to water them, and to wait for them to sprout, he will be more likely to protect them as they grow.

Effective behavior training of young children requires that the adults in the home agree on broad guidelines of conduct and that they follow what they have established. Here are some suggestions for guidelines that are consistent with Montessori principles:

- Instead of reacting to misbehavior in anger, it is much more respectful and effective to use a calm and firm voice.

- When a child misbehaves never call him "bad," "lazy," "mean" etc. Label the deed, and remind the child of appropriate behavior. "It was wrong for you to hit your brother. Remember, hands are for helping."

- Physical punishment not only demeans a child's self respect; it can make him feel that he, too, has the right to hurt other people.

- Empty threats are ineffective and will teach your child that you do not mean what you say. "Come here immediately or I will go out and leave you in the house by yourself," is not something you are likely to do, so don't use it as a threat.

- More appropriate responses to continual misbehavior are: "time out" on a chair in an uninteresting corner of the room; deprivation of such desirables as dessert, a toy, an opportunity to play, or to go out for a treat.

Do's and Don'ts for Discipline

INSTEAD OF	**TRY**
Angry shouting	A calm and firm voice
"You're a bad boy"	"Biting your sister was a very bad thing to do."
Physical punishment	A time out chair, or loss of a treat
Empty threats	Creativity, humor or a realistic consequence
Frequent rewards	Letting good behavior be the regular expectation
Allowing children to make decisions for which they lack wisdom or sufficient information	Offering 2-3 appropriate choices for children to select from
Measuring love according to behavior	Unconditional love

- If you continually reward your child for good behavior, you teach him to expect a payment for following the rules. Let good behavior be a regular expectation rather than a special occurrence that has to be recognized.

- Distractions can be a very powerful and effective tool. Some behavioral situations can best be handled with creativity or humor. When you have a two or three year-old who will not stop crying (e.g. because she could not go to a birthday party with her older sister) hold a spoon or a small cup against her cheek and tell her you want to collect her tears. "Please make some more tears for me." Inevitably her crying will stop.

- Despite their protests, children want and need firm guidance. Appropriate limits actually help a child to feel safe. Never allow your children to make decisions for which they lack experience and wisdom, such as how much TV they can watch, how much fast food they can eat, when they should go to bed, or which school they should attend. It is not unusual for a child to test your limits. Your consistent response is the most effective way to reduce testing behavior.

- You can be confident in guiding a child only if your disciplinary actions rest on a foundation of unconditional love. This means that you sincerely love your child no matter what, especially no matter what she does. It is not always easy to give unconditional love, especially at a time when you may be horrified by her behavior. Yet this kind of love is the most vital nourishment for your child's psyche. *Of all things,* Montessori proclaims, *love is the most potent...Therefore we must study it and use it, more than any of the other forces that surround us.*[62]

Showing Your Love to Young Children

In The <u>Secret of Childhood</u>, Montessori wrote convincingly about the great love the child has for the adult, a love that is not always reciprocated. *In the evening when he goes to bed, a child calls the person he loves and does not like to see him go...We defend ourselves against this love, and we shall never find another like it! We say restlessly, "I don't have the time! I can't! I'm busy."*[63]

Children are burning with love for their mothers and fathers and are hungry for love in return. Nearly all parents love their children and yet many children do not feel loved. Perhaps the reason for this is that some parents express their love with impersonal gestures, such as constantly buying things for their children, driving them to organized activities, or giving in to their every whim.

In his book, <u>How to Really Love Your Child</u>, the child psychiatrist, Dr. Ross Campbell, advises parents that they can best show love to their children by keeping their children's emotional tanks full with frequent eye contact, physical contact, and focused attention. Loving eye contact can begin with the infant. It is a continuously effective way of expressing love to your child while you are talking to her. Some parents use eye contact only when scolding a child. This practice actually discourages children from looking directly at others when speaking.

If parents are basically gentle, happy, well-adjusted adults, then their physical interactions with their children will foster emotional stability. As such a parent, you will instinctively give your children loving, yet wholesome, non-sexual physical contact—keeping an infant close to your body, holding a toddler on your lap, sharing lots of hugs, giving piggy-back rides, carrying a child on your shoulders, lifting (but not throwing) her up in the air, swinging him around and wrestling when your child is ready for this. Dr. Campbell believes that such physical expression is "crucial" to healthy psychological development.

Giving your child focused attention is the third way Dr. Campbell urges both mothers and fathers to express their love to a child— telling a story, reading to her, playing ball, making brownies, building a birdhouse, flying a kite, or any other one-on-one activity. It is difficult for children in daycare, or even in large families, to get enough of this individual attention unless their parents make a deliberate effort to give it to them. This effort requires a sacrifice of your time because you may sense that your child is in need of this focused attention at a time when you are least able to give it. Dr. Campbell cautions parents that, "without focused attention, a child experiences increased anxiety because he feels that everything else is more important than he is."[64]

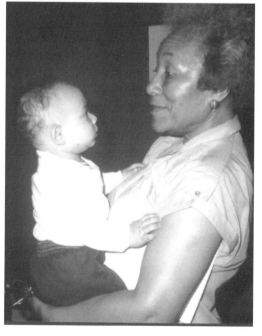

Dr. Campbell found that the best way to give focused attention is to set aside time to spend alone with each of your children. This means giving "time alone" priority in your schedule that may already be totally crammed. When our children were young my husband and I alternated in taking one child at a time out to dinner or Sunday breakfast. We also allowed each child to take turns staying up one half hour longer than the other children to play a game with either one of us. These special times occurred only because we planned them and put them on the calendar well in advance. Each event with one child was well worth the time it took from our other activities. It may have been one of the best strategies we used in many years of parenting.

If it is impossible for you to give your child enough focused attention, then try to arrange for her/him to spend a few hours with a grandparent, relative or family friend who may allow your child to join in a one-on-one activity such as gardening, handiwork, baking, playing cards, doing puzzles, or painting. I have fond memories of spending time with my aunt who allowed me to make pancakes and actually flip them on the griddle. She also showed me how to sew patches from my old dresses to make a quilt for my doll. The times I spent with her are some of my fondest memories.

There will be some days, perhaps many days, when time alone with one child is not possible for you, but there will be some days when it is possible. If you understand how important these experiences are for your child, you will make an effort to let them happen as often as possible.

Spiritual Nurturing

One of Maria Montessori's most cherished beliefs is that we can help to improve the future of human beings by nurturing the spirit of each child in our care. *The child is endowed with unknown powers, which can guide us to a radiant future. If what we really want is a new world, then education must take as its aim the development of these hidden possibilities.*[65] This, she believed, was the most important thrust of her life-long efforts on behalf of the child. When Montessori talked about nourishing the child's spirit, she was referring, I believe, to preserving the delicate inner core that holds each child's secret for a meaningful life.

Nurturing spirituality in children is very different from teaching them to observe a specific religion. Spirituality is a basic human energy that gives meaning to our lives. Religion is the way that various people choose to express their spirituality; but spirituality also resides in people who are not members of an organized religion. You can think of spirituality as an underground stream that can lift any religious practice or any way of living to a higher level.

Although Montessori referred frequently to the child's spirit in her writings, she never actually defined it. Because it is difficult to express spirit or spirituality in a brief definition, I prefer to look at how other writers have described it.

Some writers say it refers to an awareness of our sacred connection with all of life and to the oneness of the universe. Others see it as our inner life that we become aware of during periods of silence. Some speak of it as a feeling of awe and reverence that comes when contemplating nature. Many feel that spirituality gives us depth—a depth that enables us to see that we are called to a greater purpose than self-service or self-satisfaction. Others say it leads us to sharing rather than accumulating, cooperation rather than constant competition, peace rather than violence. All these descriptions, I believe, are significant aspects of spirituality.

Many parents, wondering how they can instill spiritual awareness in their children, are surprised to learn that it is already there. Montessori believed that each child is gifted with a natural spiritual sense. When she picks up a worm, pulls apart a daisy, or chases a butterfly, a child is showing us little miracles of life that we have long since taken for granted. As Jean Grasso Fitzpatrick writes, "The greatest challenge we all face as spiritual nurturers is to become attuned to the young child's authentic spirituality, which—unlike our own—is still such an integrated part of life…Children's exuberant spirituality is reflected in everything they do…A child shows us the extraordinary in the ordinary."[66] The task of parents, therefore, is to respect and protect this wondrous gift by nurturing each sign of its presence and creating conditions in which it can flourish.

One means of doing this is to give your children some experience of silence in a world filled with the constant noise of traffic, TV, radio and all kinds of motorized appliances. Prepare a special corner in your home where a child could sit quietly, looking at a fish bowl or a collection of shells or stones. *Silence,* says Montessori, *often brings us the knowledge …that we possess within ourselves an interior life.* [67]

You can also take your three or four year-old outside and suggest that you both sit quietly, eyes closed with no one saying a word.

Your child may tell you afterwards "I heard the birds singing" or "I heard the wind blowing all the leaves." You may also enjoy times of quiet together while you look at a fire burning, watch waves coming on to a beach, or simply gaze at the reflection of the sky and trees in a pond.

Another aspect of spiritual nurturing is encouraging your children to be close to nature, thus fostering their sense of awe and wonder. *In the civilized environment of our society*, Montessori says, *children live far from nature, and have few opportunities of entering into intimate contact with it. Does anyone,* she asks, *let them run out when it is raining, take off their shoes when they find pools of water, and let them run about with bare feet when the grass...is damp with dew?*[88]

Taking a walk with your child, even if it is only in your own garden, gives him delightful opportunities to explore nature. He will enjoy watching butterflies, noticing bees visiting flowers, looking at a colony of ants building an ant hill, or being surprised at all the life teeming beneath a rotting log that you have turned over.

My daughter told me she took a "garden walk" with a child she frequently babysat as part of their "Night, night" routine. They said hello or goodnight to all the plants by name. It could last from five to fifteen minutes and was a lovely time together.

Going for a longer walk inevitably points to the necessity of taking the child's pace. *The child is not trying to 'get there'. All he wants is to walk,*[69] to stop and pick dandelions or to splash in a puddle. In the fall, take a container with you so he can gather acorns, horse chestnuts or colored leaves. In the spring look for all the activity around a bird's nest and the miracle of plants that are sprouting. "Could you grow that much in one week? How did the little plant do that?"

There are many activities you can put in a spiritual perspective. For example, if your children are planting seeds in little containers, have them set aside one carefully marked container in which they plant only a button or a penny. Place this container, with the others, in a sunny spot and water all of them carefully. The lack of a result in this container will increase their admiration for the remarkable power of life in the seeds in the other containers.

For a special treat on a clear night, take your child outside to a darkened area and look at the sky together. Tell him, "This is our universe. It is the biggest thing we have, and you and I are part of it."

Parents can also help children to express gratitude for all the gifts of nature that enable us to live on the earth, especially for the sun that gives us light and warmth, for water, for our food, our home and our family. A grace before meals, and thanksgiving for loved ones at bedtime, are other ways of nurturing gratitude.

Wonder and gratitude lead to a sense of love and respect for the earth and her creatures. Even very young children can care for the earth in simple ways, such as picking up trash, conserving water, and putting items in your recycling bin. They also enjoy filling the bird-feeder, replenishing water bowls for the pets, and watering indoor plants or the garden.

Children as young as three can be encouraged to act peacefully, and to help others with such kindnesses as helping to clean up water that has spilled, or assisting a younger sibling to put on his boots. Steven R. Covey, the author of The 7 Habits of Highly Effective People, once wrote this advice to parents: "I think that the most significant work we ever do, in our whole world, in our whole life, is done within the four walls of our own home. All mothers and fathers, whatever their stations in life, can make the most significant of contributions by imprinting the spirit of service on the souls of their children, so that the children grow up committed to making a difference."[70] Helping others can begin in the earliest years!

Joy, too, is an expression of children's spirituality. In my book, Nurturing the Spirit in Non-Sectarian Classrooms, I wrote, "While spiritual nurture always includes periods of quiet and solitude it must also frequently erupt in expressions of joy. Singing, dancing, painting, pretending, constructing, playing with puppets, imagining characters while listening to a story are all expressions of children's joy. I particularly feel the human spirit in the exuberance of song and dance. Why not dance more with children? Not necessarily formal dancing, just moving spontaneously to the rhythm of beautiful music. What else says so clearly that it is good to be alive? Dancing and all the other arts allow children to express their inner spirituality with the joy that is such a natural element of childhood."[71]

If religion is part of your family tradition, do not hesitate to share some of the signs of your faith with your children. At a young age, a child can feel great awe in a temple, a mosque, a church or a chapel where she becomes aware of a sacred atmosphere, different from the outside world, lighted perhaps by stained glass windows, or beautiful candles. Religious ceremonies also speak the child's sensorial language, as she smells incense, feels holy water and/or listens to sacred music. Even if a child does not fully understand a religious service, attendance can give her a sense of the mystery hidden within everyday life.

Montessori in Today's Family

Using Montessori principles at home in the 21st century can seem like swimming against giant waves of fast foods, tight schedules, incessant TV, computers, electronic toys, and organized sports for children as young as four. Parents who allow these commercially inspired entities to invade their family life may find that these aspects of popular culture actually work against the positive outcomes they desire for their children. What are these outcomes?

Nearly all parents want their children to be healthy, to be well educated, to have good friends, meaningful work, to be happy, to be virtuous and to be wise. What many parents don't realize however, is that the essential foundation for these auspicious outcomes begins in the child's earliest years. Many of the results depend on your early choices—whether you eat nutritious or convenience foods, whether your children have beneficial exercise or long periods of sitting, whether your children can play imaginatively with friends or only in an organized group, whether they are close to nature or to electronic gadgets, whether they are frequently read to or constantly watching television.

To reduce the power of the disturbing influences that swamp children's lives almost unnoticed, I suggest that parents plan their resistance when their first child is born or whenever they become aware of this helpful strategy. Make a list of the values that you hold most dear. Add the steps you will take to live these values and the deterring influences you will avoid. When you put these goals on paper, you will strengthen your resolve to maintain your personal values in our fast moving, commercially driven world. In his very practical book, The Intentional Family, William J. Doherty, Ph.D., writes, "An Intentional Family is one whose members create a working plan for maintaining and building family ties, and then implement the plan as best they can. An Intentional Family rows and steers its boat rather than being moved only by the winds and the current."[72]

Listing your desired outcomes in this way does not mean that you determine a career, a college, or even a hobby for your child. A child's passion that may eventually lead to meaningful work is a precious personal desire that must not be unduly influenced or squelched by powerful adults. *As I have so often said*, Montessori wrote, *it is true we cannot make a genius. We can only give to each individual the chance to fulfill his or her unique potential.*[73]

The greatest opportunity for you to do this is when your child is in the first plane of human development. *At no other age has the child greater need of intelligent help, and any obstacle that impedes his creative work will lessen the chance he has of reaching his potential. We should help the child, therefore, no longer because we think of him as a creature, puny and weak, but because he is endowed with great creative energies.*[74] To these energies parents can give the most loving and nurturing assistance. This was true when Montessori proclaimed its importance and it is still one of the most consequential aspects of parenting in the 21st century.

End Notes

[1]   *The Absorbent Mind.* p. 14.
[2]   ibid. p. 4.
[3]   ibid. p. 195.
[4]   ibid. p. 162.
[5]   ibid. p. 24.
[6]   *The First Three Years of Life.* p. 4.
[7]   *To Educate The Human Potential.* p. 4.
[8]   *The Absorbent Mind.* p. 21.
[9]   *Erkinder.* p. 9.
[10] ibid. p. 6.
[11] ibid. p. 15.
[12] *The Absorbent Mind.* p. 22.
[13] ibid. pp. 4-6.
[14] ibid. pp. 16-17.
[15] ibid. p. 98.
[16] ibid. p. 99.
[17] ibid. p. 97.
[18] ibid. p. 103.
[19] ibid. pp. 153-54.
[20] ibid. p. 24.
[21] ibid. p. 24.
[22] ibid. p. 105.
[23] ibid. p. 73.
[24] *The Secret of Childhood. (1962).* p. 113.
[25] *The Absorbent Mind.* p. 142.
[26] ibid. p. 161.
[27] ibid. p. 161.
[28] ibid. p. 83.
[29] ibid. p. 84.

30   ibid. p. 89.

31   ibid. pp. 90-91.

32   ibid. p. 155.

33   ibid. p. 190.

34   ibid. p. 126.

35   *The Secret of Childhood* (Fides 1966).   p. 65.

36   *The Read Aloud Handbook.* p. 128.

37   ibid. p. 17.

38   ibid. p. 44.

39   ibid. p. xxiii.

40   *The Absorbent Mind.* p. 160.

41   ibid. p. 222.

42   ibid. p. 27; p. 148; p. 151.

43   ibid. p. 150.

44   ibid. p. 152; p. 155.

45   *The Secret of Childhood.* (India) p. 217.

46   *The Absorbent Mind.* p. 30.

47   ibid. p. 156.

48   *Look at the Child.* p. 62.

49   *The Absorbent Mind.* p. 101.

50   *Endangered Minds.* p. 198.

51   *The Absorbent Mind.* p. 27.

52   *The Read Aloud Handbook.* p. 203.

53   *The Absorbent Mind.* p. 37.

54   *Evolution's End.* pp. 164; 165.

55   <u>Pediatrics</u> Magazine, April 2004.

56   *The Read Aloud Handbook.* p. 197.

57   *The Hidden Heart of the Cosmos.* p. 132.

58   *Endangered Minds.* pp. 219-220.

59   ibid. p. 225.

60   *The Absorbent Mind.* p. 254.

61   ibid. p. 258.

62   ibid. p. 295.

63   *The Secret of Childhood* (Fides). pp. 127-128.

64   *How to Really Love Your Child.* p. 60.

65   *The Absorbent Mind.* p. 4.

66   *Something More, Nurturing Your Child's Spiritual Growth.* p. 45.

67   *Maria Montessori, Her Life and Work* (paperback). p. 226.

68   *The Discovery of the Child.* p. 98; p. 100.

69   *The Absorbent Mind.* p. 162.

70   *Handbook for the Soul.* p. 143.

71   *Nurturing the Spirit in Non-Sectarian Classrooms.* p. 149.

72   *The Intentional Family.* p. 8.

73   *The Absorbent Mind.* p. 94.

74   ibid. p. 28.

Bibliography and
Suggested Reading for Parents

Campbell, Dr. Ross. *How To Really Love Your Child.* Wheaton IL: Victor Books, 1977. A very helpful perspective for maximizing the quality of parent-child relationships by a psychiatrist who specializes in working with young children. Currently out of print but worth searching for in libraries or out of print dealers on the web.

Carlson, Richard and Benjamin Shield. *Handbook for the Soul.* Boston MA: Little, Brown and Company 1995.

Chilton Pearce, Joseph. *Evolutions' End.* San Francisco: Harper, 1992.

Covey, Stephen R. The 7 *Habits of Highly Effective Families.* New York: Golden Books, 1997. This book shows how you can make your family a priority in a turbulent world, moving from problem solving to accomplishing goals.

Doherty, William J. Ph.D. *The Intentional Family—Simple Rituals to Strengthen Family Ties.* New York: Harper Collins, 1997. Useful guidelines that will help you to make the most of your most important relationships using proven strategies for reviving a lost sense of family.

Fitzpatrick, Jean Grasso. *Something More, Nurturing Your Child's Spiritual Growth.* New York; Viking, 1991. This is an inspiring and practical approach to raising a child with a sense of meaning and purpose in an uncertain world.

Healy, Jane M. Ph.D. *Endangered Minds.* New York: Simon and Schuster, 1990. Dr. Healy examines the reasons why children today are less able to concentrate and less able "to think" than preceding generations.

Montessori, Maria. *The Absorbent Mind.* New York: Henry Holt and Company, 1995.

_____. *To Educate the Human Potential.* Adyar, Madras, India: Kalakshetra Publications, 1948.

_____. *The Secret of Childhood.* Hyderabad, India: Orient Longman 1962 and Notre Dame IN; Fides Publishers, Inc., 1966.

_____. *Erkinder.* Battersea, UK: The Maria Montessori Training Organization.

_____. *The Discovery of the Child.* Madras, India: Kalakshetra Publications, 1958.

Severe, Sal Ph.D. *How to Behave So Your Children Will Too!* New York: Viking Penguin, 2000. This book shows why a child's behavior is often a reflection of the parents' behavior, and how, by making changes themselves, parents can achieve dramatic results in their children.

Standing, E.M. *Maria Montessori Her Life and Work.* New York: American Library, 1962.

Swimme, Brian. *The Hidden Heart of the Cosmos.* Maryknoll NY: Orbis Books, 1999.

Trelese, Jim. *The Read Aloud Handbook.* New York: Penguin Books, 2001. A genuine classic, now in its fifth edition—an inspiration for parents and teachers backed by up to date research and a list of over 1500 age-appropriate books for children.

White, Burton. *The First Three Years of Life.* Englewood Cliffs, NJ: Prentice-Hall, Inc., 1975.

Wolf, Aline D. *Nurturing the Spirit in Non-Sectarian Classrooms.* Altoona, PA: Parent Child Press, Inc., 1996. A guide for any parents or teachers who want to include the spiritual dimension in their care of young children.

_____. *Look at the Child.* Hollidaysburg, PA: Parent Child Press, Inc. 1974.

About Maria Montessori

Maria Montessori (1870-1952), known throughout the world as the originator of the Montessori Method of Education, was the first woman in Italy to receive a medical degree. In 1902, while working with retarded and disturbed children, she was inspired to design a variety of learning materials which proved very successful with these handicapped children.

Her opportunity to have these materials used by a larger and more diverse group of children came in 1907 when she started a pre-school project for socially disadvantaged children in the San Lorenzo district of Rome. Her Casa dei Bambini, or Children's House, became world famous; educational observers came from many different countries to watch the young children absorbed in learning with these unusual materials. Eventually Montessori gave up her medical practice and devoted her life to training teachers, writing and lecturing for any adults who cared for children. Her schools, that are still flourishing, have spread to six continents.

The most important thrust of all her educational efforts was to create a more peaceful world by nurturing the spirit of children. For this unusual approach to peace she was nominated three times for the Nobel Peace Prize.

About Aline Wolf

Aline Wolf has long been regarded as a modern interpreter of Maria Montessori's philosophy and methods. In 1961 with her husband, Gerald, she founded Penn-Mont Academy, the first Montessori school to be licensed in Pennsylvania and the third in the nation. Her best-known book, *A Parents' Guide to the Montessori Classroom*, is now a classic in the Montessori world and has been translated into Spanish, Swedish and Chinese. In subsequent books, Aline highlighted Montessori's insights for parenting, and for teaching peace. She also developed an art appreciation program for young children featuring a manual and a series of art postcard books entitled *Child-Size Masterpieces*.

With the publication of her pivotal book, *Nurturing the Spirit in Non-Sectarian Classrooms*, she narrowed her focus to the most important aspect of all Montessori's educational work—attaining peace by nurturing the spirit of the child. Recent publications include a series of Cosmic Wonder Books for children and *I Wonder What's Out There, a Vision of the Universe for Primary Classes*, that she co-authored with Joanne Alex.

Other Titles Available from Parent Child Press

By Aline Wolf:
 A Parents' Guide to the Montessori Classroom (available in Spanish)
 Nurturing the Spirit in Non-Sectarian Classrooms (available in Spanish)
 Our Peaceful Classroom
 Look at the Child
 The World of the Child
 Andy and His Daddy
 Cosmic Wonder Series (six small books for children)
 Thoughtful Living Series (six small books for children)
 Child-Size Masterpieces for Art Appreciation
  How to Use Child-size Masterpieces for Art Appreciation
  Easy: Level 1 for Steps 1,2 & 3
  Intermediate: Level 2 for Steps 1,2 & 3
  Advanced: Level 3 for Steps 1,2 & 3
  Step 4: Learning the Names of the Artists
  Step 5: Learning about Famous Paintings
  Steps 6 & 7: Modern Schools of Art
  Step 8: Transportation in America
  Black Images

By Joanne DeFillipp Alex with Aline Wolf:
 I Wonder What's Out There
By Michael and D'Neil Duffy:
 Children of the Universe
 Math Works
By Alicia Jewell:
 The Peace Rose
By Joan Gilbert:
 Sense of Wonder Series (six early reading booklets)
By Joe Servello:
 You Are An Artist
By Gerald Wolf:
 Transportation in America (art postcards for a timeline)

www.parentchildpress.com